BEYOND
OUR
COCOONS

"Just do the steps that you've been shown
By everyone you've ever known
Until the dance becomes your very own . . ."

~Jackson Browne~

Just imagine for a moment . . .

You're trudging through life,
pretty much playing by the rules,
but feeling less than fulfilled,
striving yet never quite arriving,
and wondering if this is all an illusion,
getting tired of doing the same dance,
and considering dancing
down a different road.

Then you stumble upon a magic
flashing button that reads,
in small print,
"Press here for a change."

You're tempted. You hesitate.
You debate. You contemplate.
Then you close your eyes,
take the deepest of breaths
and press it . . .

and . . . .

. . . you find yourself exactly
where you are right now,
about to read this little book.

Ready?

Life is a great surprise to the newly-born me. I came from nowhere to now here. My dance of life has begun. This should be great.

An adventure awaits me. I'm
excited, innocent and eager to be
just me.

But I soon find out it's hard being just me. That's not what's expected.

I'm taught how to be. I'm told what I can and can't be in this dance of life.

My great adventure changes. It must follow a well-traveled road. I learn to do the dance of life that I'm shown–not my own. I can't be the real me that way.

I get in trouble when the real me shows up doing a different dance of life. So I wear a mask to hide the real me and my real dance.

I sometimes take off the mask
and let the real me show.

**Without the mask I get hurt
cause I'm not the me others
expect me to be.**

So I wear the mask and try to do the dance I'm shown. With the mask on, my parents and teachers like me better.

The more I wear the mask, the less I know myself. So, unable to do my own dance, the real me suffers and grows depressed.

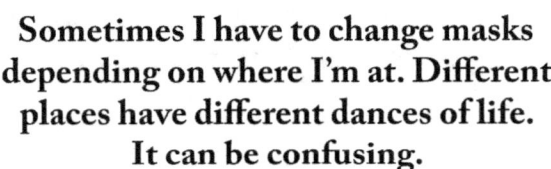

Sometimes I have to change masks
depending on where I'm at. Different
places have different dances of life.
It can be confusing.

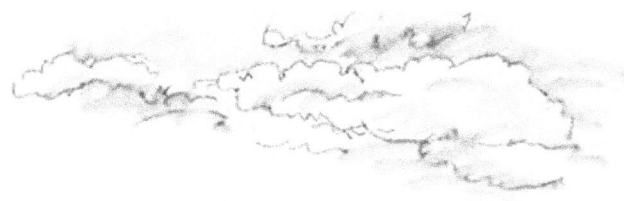

I have masks for home, for church and for other places. Sometimes I wear the wrong one. Then I'm in trouble again.

The masks often confuse me.
Sometimes I lose my balance and
fall. This hurts. The real me shows
when the masks come off.

I know the real me can't grow
like this so I hide even more behind
bigger masks. I'm afraid others might
see the real me and not like the tiny me.

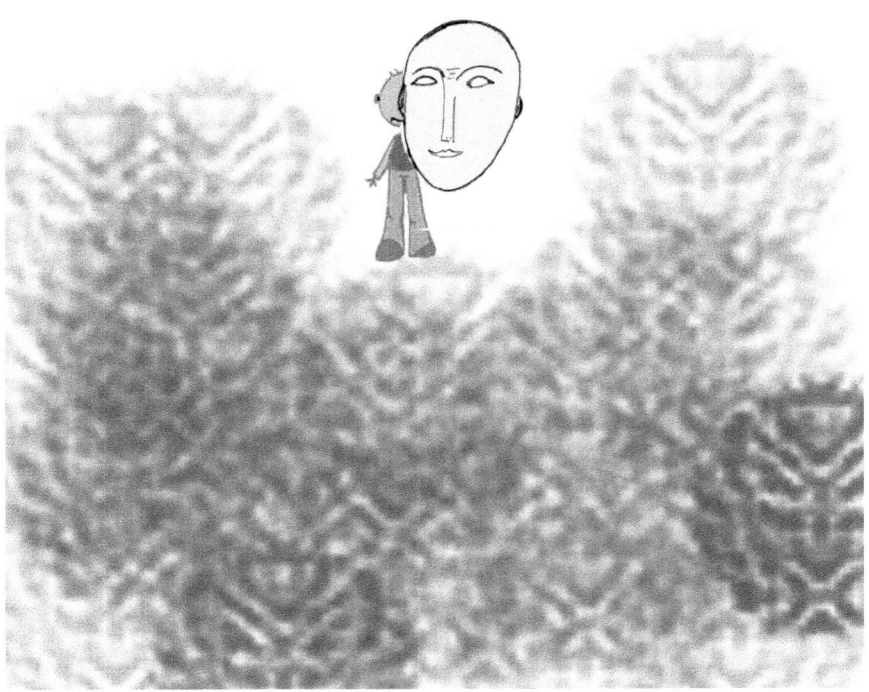

So gradually the masks become
things that the real me is not.

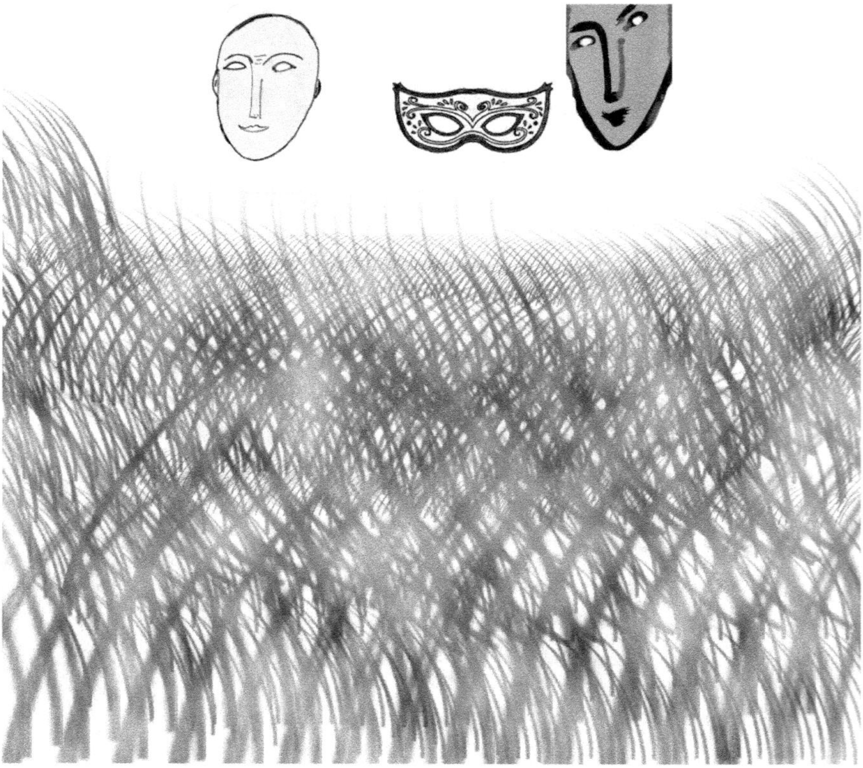

The masks keep growing and
I don't–not the real me anyway.

The masks get so big it becomes hard to put them on. Soon I'm using most of my energy to keep them in place.

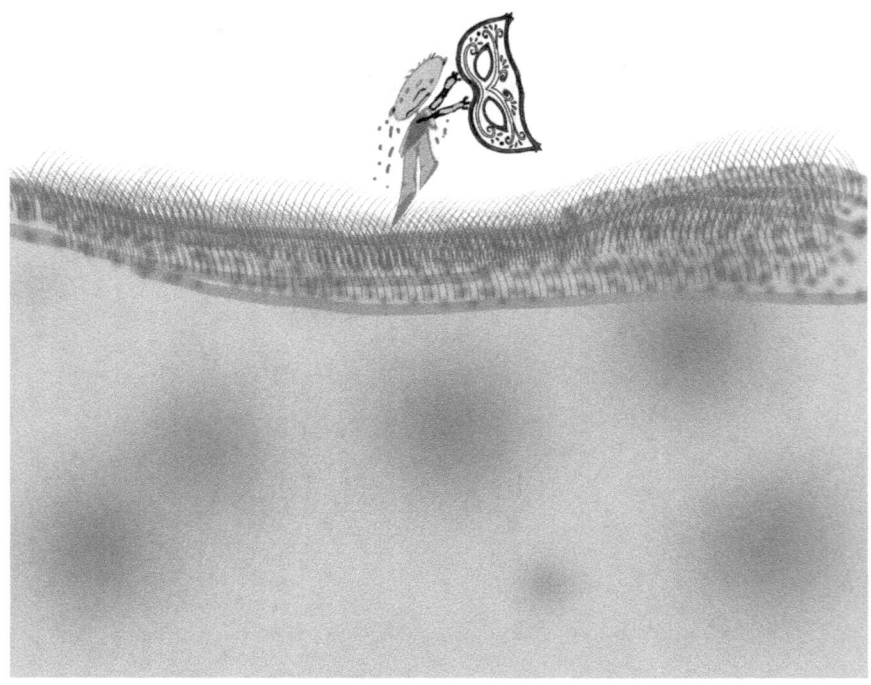

The heavy masks leave me with
less energy to find myself–to be
the real me. Slowly, the masks
begin to control my life.

But I get in trouble if I
don't do the dance and wear
the heavy masks. So I wear one
most all the time. I want to be good.

I get so used to a mask
that I rarely ever take it off.
I might sometimes when I'm
alone because I feel safer then.
But I wonder who I'm becoming
behind my masks. Do I
even know myself?

I worry about my masks
getting so heavy that I might
drop and break them. Where
would I hide the real me then?

When I've worn the masks
long enough, it seems like
they are me, even though I know
full well they are not.

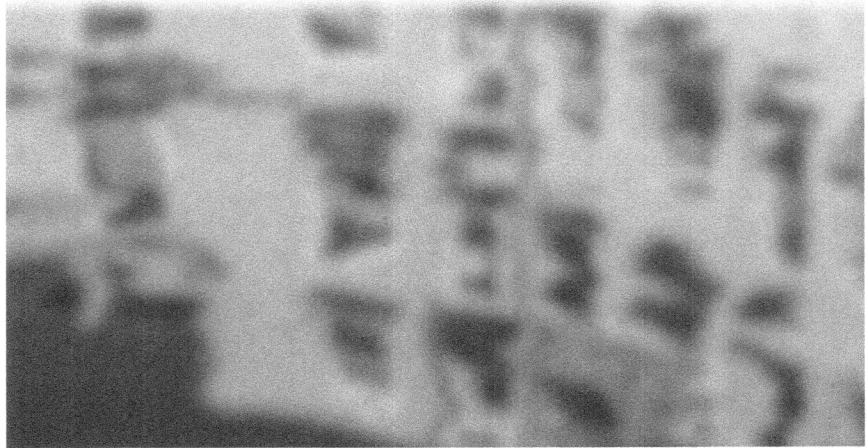

One day I met a girl I liked
a lot. Her name was Jocelyn and
her mask looked much like
mine. I complimented her on
her mask. She liked mine too.
I smiled behind my mask.

We took long walks and
had long talks but always wore
our masks. I think I was falling
in love with this girl.

I took her home and to church, both of us wearing our masks. As I got to know her, I wondered if she liked me or only my mask. Would she like the real me–the person behind the mask?

We danced in exotic places
and became close—almost
inseparable. But our masks were
always on. I thought
nothing of it at first.

But in quiet moments, I wondered if she really liked me or only my mask. She'd never seen the real me and my mask was much the same as hers.

My mask

Her mask

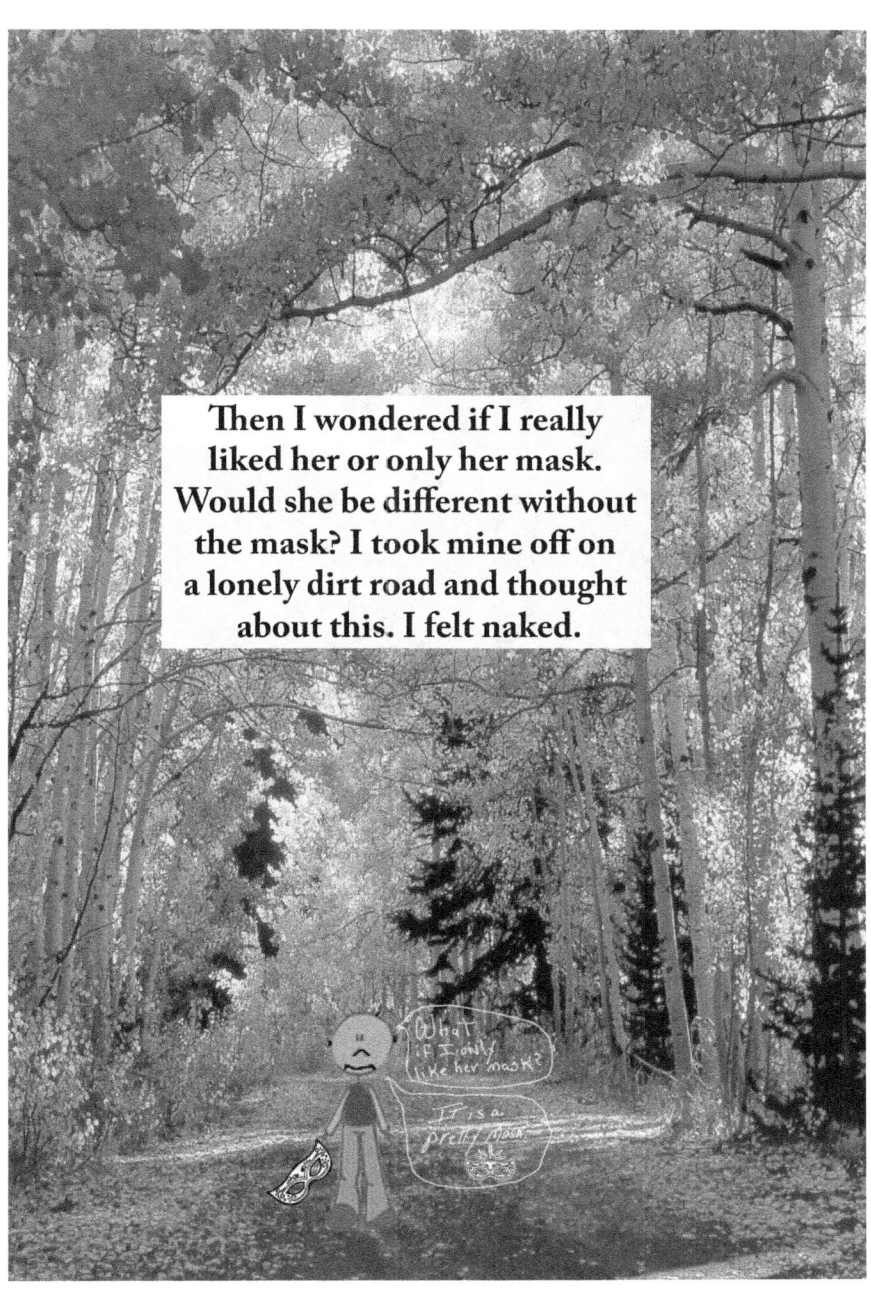

Then I wondered if I really liked her or only her mask. Would she be different without the mask? I took mine off on a lonely dirt road and thought about this. I felt naked.

I started to hate the masks.
I didn't know who I was. Was
I the mask? Was the mask me?
Where was my very own self–
my very own dance of life?

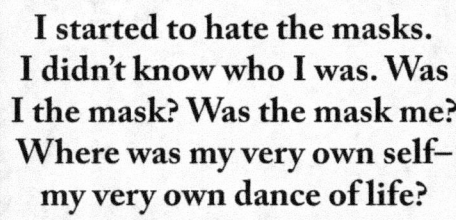

I realized I would
only know the real
me when I knew the
mask wasn't me.

I was becoming lost
in a fog of uncertainty.
I knew something must change.

One day while walking a butterfly landed on my mask. It said, "Why do you stay in your cocoon? You'll enjoy things more without it. Let me show you."

The butterfly took me to its cocoon.
I was amazed—the cocoon even looked
a little like my mask. Most importantly,
I could see the real beauty of the
butterfly without its cocoon-mask. It
was free. It could fly its own dance.
The butterfly told me even more
secrets about masks and things.

He said, "Without
change there would
be no butterflies."

After learning from the butterfly, I got rid of my mask. It was scary at first but felt good and uplifting. Then I decided to help others put down their masks. The whole world looked better too.

My girlfriend liked me even
without the mask. Now I got
her love and attention rather than
my mask getting it. That felt great.
I could see clearly now.

She saw how happy I was without a mask. She said she wanted to take hers off too but was afraid to do it. She asked if I would help her.

I held her hand as I told her about
the butterfly's secret. The butterfly said
he used his cocoon mask to develop some
but had to leave it to fully develop–to
spread its wings and fly. Some don't leave
the cocoon. Their wings don't develop and
most growth stops. In the cocoon mask, they
never live the full life of a developed
butterfly. They never discover what they
could be. They never fly. Their color and
grace are never seen. Even worse, they
don't get to see the world. The cocoon mask
hides much of it from them–they never
find their true place in the world. The cocoon
becomes their world and they never get
to rise to their potential. Most importantly
the butterfly said, "Every one has a rightful
place and once it is found, it is beautiful.
But you'll never find it wearing a mask."

I told her she needed to protect
her true self from the self the world
wanted her to be. "You can't do that
wearing a mask."

And that, "I wanted to love her
and not just her mask."

I must have said something right.
She threw her mask high in a tree.

And for the very first time, I saw
her beautiful eyes, her
long blond hair and her full smile.

Since unmasking we've both grown. We no longer do the dance we were shown by most everyone we had known. Instead we do a dance now that's our very own.

And the two of them lived and danced "maskless" ever after.

"Be yourself; everybody else is taken."

~Oscar Wilde~